52 Tips for Owning Your Career

Practical Advice for Career Success

SIMONE E. MORRIS

Simone Morris Enterprises LLC
304 Main Avenue, #379
Norwalk, CT 06851
www.simonemorrisenterprises.org

Ordering Information
Quantity sales. Special discounts are available on
quantity purchases by corporations,
associations, and others. For details, contact the
publisher at the address above.

You may also order copies at
www.simonemorrisenterprises.org/shop

Printed in the United States of America

DEDICATION

Someone recently said to me, "Success leaves crumbs." This book is my version of crumbs for the next generation.

I dedicate this book to my daughter Mildred. May this book serve as a resource to you as you take on your life's purpose. I know you will do great things, my love.

In addition, I honor my mother for her sacrifices to create a better future for our family. It is only as I age that I begin to realize the immeasurable sacrifices that you made for us. Momma B, we thank you. I love you always.

SPREAD THE LOVE

Get this book for the special people in your life. Help them to soar in their careers by taking advantage of 52 tips for career success. They will thank you for impacting their careers.

52 TIPS
FOR OWNING
YOUR CAREER

Practical Advice for Career Success

SIMONE E. MORRIS

CONTENTS

ACKNOWLEDGMENTS

I want to acknowledge my love Stephen. Thank you for loving the whole me and always cheering me on to do great things. I appreciate you. I love you.

I want to acknowledge my BFF Bridgett for the countless conversations we've had about being successful in business. She's always ready when I throw crazy ideas out to her, and for that I'm grateful. I say thank you to her often for the gift of her friendship. Thank you B for everything.

Thank you to Kim, who always converts my thoughts to beautiful visuals. I love all the work that you do and the partnership that we've formed over the years.

Thank you Joni for gifting me with your editorial talents. All I can say is, "Wow." More to come.

To Alan Douville, the Stryker's Women's Network, and the Stryker Information Systems team in Kalamazoo, Michigan, you inspired me so much during my time with you that I spent the plane ride home penning the start of this book to provide more clear instructions about how you can continue to own your careers.

To Mothers of Preschoolers (MOPS) of Wilton, Connecticut, I want to thank you for having me share my message that mothers deserve careers too. Your prayer over my message deeply touched me and confirmed to me that there was indeed more that I had to share with the world on this topic.

I want to thank everyone who's attended one of my workshops. Gaining insights about your career journey was super helpful to me as I fine-tuned my message.

Thank you to all my guests on the Power of Owning Your Career Podcast. Your sage career advice is truly appreciated.

And finally, to you my dear readers, thank you for continuing to take this journey with me. I love sharing my career experiences and practical career tips with you. I wish you continued career successes. Be sure to take your rightful place in the driver's seat.

1 INTRODUCTION

I've been on a mission to empower women to get happy with their careers and take full responsibility for the trajectory of their careers for the past six years. This was a feeling that stemmed from an upbringing in a single-parent household.

It took a number of years to move myself from the proverbial passenger seat to a consistent place in the driver's seat. First, I didn't even believe I deserved to call the shots for my career, and as such I was allowing others to do so for me. I was more of the mindset that I should be grateful for the longevity of a well-paying job with superb perks.

Having done all that, I got to the point where I wanted more for myself. I wanted to feel like I was making a significant contribution to the world. When I became disillusioned with my tenure in corporate America, I sought other avenues to create fulfillment.

Recently, a former leader asked if I told anyone that I was unhappy during my time in corporate America. My response was I didn't feel safe to share my full truth with anyone in the corporate space. I had moments where I was driven to show up more, but it was really difficult for me, given that I was taught to keep the two worlds separate. Honestly, I didn't trust the process and as such I held my cards close to the vest.

I'll always be grateful for the education, empowerment, resources, and lifelong friendships I gained from my time in corporate America as an employee. Now I fully embrace this next chapter that includes running my own business to empower others who are on a similar journey for clarity and fulfillment.

Why did I write this book?

When I wrote my first book, *Achievement Unlocked: Strategies to Set Goals and Manifest Them*, almost immediately thereafter, I had a distinct feeling that there was another story to be told. Something was urging me on to share my career journey and lessons that ultimately led me to penning the second book, *The Power of Owning Your Career*.

While I knew I wanted to write more books, I was torn about what would follow after *The Power of Owning Your Career*. I was torn on whether I wanted to write a book on Inclusive Leadership or another book on more strategies for Career Excellence and Growth.

I toiled over the path until the answer came to me loud and clear. It was after I delivered a speech at Stryker Corporation. I felt the energy and engagement of the audience. The questions being asked led me to believe that I needed to share more on exactly how to get into the driver's seat. As such, *52 Tips for Owning Your Career: Practical Advice for Career Success* was born.

How is this book different from *The Power of Owning Your Career* book?

In *The Power of Owning Your Career*, I talked about the importance of having a formula for owning your career. I shared a diverse slate of leaders who were willing to share their career journeys and lessons for success. This book, *52 Tips for Owning Your Career: Practical Advice for Career Success* takes the message one step further. More actionable advice is provided about how to achieve career success.

In this book, you will hear more of Simone's voice and experiences that aim to resonate with you as you position yourself in the driver's seat for your career.

Depicted on the next page is the current version of my eight-step power of owning your career (POOYC) formula. We will use this as a framework for garnering continued career growth.

THE POWER OF OWNING YOUR CAREER

Know that your POOYC formula doesn't have to be a replica of mine nor does it have to remain static. It will morph over time, as mine has.

STEP 1: CLAIM

The first step in my formula is understanding that I deserve to be happy in my career. I deserve to call the shots. I deserve to reach the end of life and know that my career body of work had my input firmly engrained in it. I didn't always know that and so I didn't behave in that manner. Today, I can say that I'm the CEO of my career and making choices that represent my needs and desired goals.

STEP 2: AUDIT

The second step in my formula is to continuously audit my career. I'm auditing because I don't want to rest on my laurels, and I want to pay attention to what's happening so I can be hands-on at all times. Auditing is important because it allows you to look below the surface and gain data points to make informed decisions. You need to know what's working and what's not working. Only then, can you move forward with creating greater change.

STEP 3: PLAN

The third step in the formula is having a solid plan of action for my career. Understand that to have this solid plan, you must spend a good amount of time thinking through your career desires and goals. If you don't know what you want, do some research to find out what is best for you. Observe others. Create a profile and hang out on the LinkedIn site and observe your feed for insights. If you're not getting the research you want, start to follow some new folks that you admire. Hang out in groups and observe the leaders who populate to the top. Take notes.

Notice I didn't give you a pass to remain a passenger by staying in a space where you're unsure of what you want to achieve. If you're not sure, invest the time to get clarity so you can plan accordingly for your career.

One of the key ideas I want you to keep in mind is that you have permission to do trials and errors until you figure out what's right for you. Don't give in to feeling like you have to have it perfectly figured out at all times. I got stuck in that trap, and it caused me to be stalled for a long time. I don't want that for you. Get clear and then move through the steps in the formula.

I can go into great detail about what is required in a plan. Remember I teach project management for a living. However, I know not all of us want to be expert project managers, so let me keep it simple and highlight what components have been useful to me in the format of a plan. More planning resources are available on the www.simonemorrisenterprises.org/shop website.

A career master plan should have the following.

- A list of career goals/requirements
- Defined time buckets (used for measuring success)
- Areas of focus (priority)
- Actions required to achieve your goals
- Tracking method
- Accountability partnerships defined
- Budget

There's a lot more to having a solid project plan. If you're on the advanced side, you can give some thought to potential risks and strategies for mitigating those risks. If you want to learn more about project management, you can visit www.pmi.org.

The investment I made in getting educated on project management principles has served me well in my career. Honestly, this education has been game-changing. No matter what fields I have pursued, I have been able to leverage my training on project management. I'm particularly tickled about how much of the learning I'm using in my current role.

STEP 4: PERFORM

It seems like a no-brainer to suggest that you have to do work to get results. I state it because many people are going through life with the misconception that things can happen without doing the requisite work. Hence, I'm here to remind anyone reading this book that you must take consistent action to realize your goals. Plain and simple, this is about doing the work to be successful. You cannot expect to rest on your laurels or leave the wheel to someone else. Taking consistent action will ensure you are accountable to yourself but also to others.

STEP 5: PARTNER

The next step in my formula is about partnering. I know that success is a team sport. I fully believe it, but there was a time when I was resistant to help. I really felt like I could do it on my own **or** even worse, I felt like I didn't have to ask for help. I thought people would just willingly help me. I was greatly disappointed when I learned otherwise.

I'm blessed to have had some wonderful partners along my career journey. I just didn't realize that I needed more partners on my team. Part of this partnering process includes input from the audit process. Once I'm able to identify gaps in my expertise, then I know where I need partners to support me.

Going back to *The Power of Owning Your Career* book, I reference the power of having a sponsor as one of the key partnerships to leverage in owning your career. I still believe strongly in the sponsor concept. I've also heard it from other leaders. They use terms like advocate, champion, etc. The key is to have others vying for your career success. Sponsors don't have to only come from senior management roles. However, those folks generally have the power to make things happen.

Take time to get clear about your career goals and identify people you need to help you succeed. Then you can go about engaging them to join your success board. By the way, you might not know who you need immediately but be sure to adjust your plans along the way.

STEP 6: PROMOTE

The next step is about the power of having a personal brand. A brand that you're proud to promote. We must be the ones who are tooting our horns about our career achievements, possibilities, and even challenges. Let the world know what you're capable of. This is a must in my book.

If you're one of those people under the illusion that your work alone will speak for itself, think again. I've had introverts come up to me after I have spoken and confide that they have difficulties tooting their own horn. I can relate, having been there.

A recent article at *US News and World Report*, penned by Robin Madell, spoke to the struggles that women have tooting their own horns for fear of being seen as conceited or boastful. Ms. Madell speaks about a survey conducted of 1,000 professional women wherein almost 85 percent of those surveyed felt uncomfortable tooting their horns.

In this day and age of competition, you cannot afford **not** to be your best public relations person. You must share your successes. You must embrace the uncomfortableness of it until you get more comfortable. I recommend keeping an eye on promoting your personal brand. It takes time to get clear on what your personal brand is.

STEP 7: SELF-CARE

Self-care is vital for career success. Burnout is real. Stay fueled so you can persevere on your career journey. Be sure to make yourself a priority. This means taking time to care for yourself mentally, physically, and spiritually. Shortchanging yourself on any of these areas will undoubtedly stall your progress.

Take a car as an analogy. When the car is empty, the car sputters along. If you invest in upkeep for your car, it runs along smoothly. That means regular oil changes. Regular service visits. Continuing to gas up when required. Washing the car and giving it a good detail keeps up the outer body of the vehicle.

Can you see how important it is to take good care of yourself?

Book time on your calendar for your self-care and hold yourself accountable for ensuring your well-being is in order. Make time for wellness, physical regimen, fun in your life, family, friendships, and sleep.

STEP 8: CELEBRATE

We must take time out of our busy lives to celebrate successes along this journey. Don't breeze by each accomplishment with a readiness for what's next. Do something nice for yourself. Acknowledge your hard work. Buy yourself something special. Treat yourself to a nice dinner and go ahead and get some ice cream for dessert. You've earned it. Let your celebration be as sweet as the victory.

What happens when you own your career (that is, you are in the driver's seat for your career)?

When you are in the driver's seat for your career, there is a sense of peace and knowingness that you were a ready, willing, and able participant. You feel fully vested in all decisions related to your career. You realize that at any given point, you're empowered to make decisions that are in your best interest. You understand that you can say no to opportunities that don't make sense for your personal brand.

Those in the driver's seat have a plan for their careers. They know it takes a team to succeed, and they are willing to go the extra mile to create relationships for success. Those in the driver's seat have learned that there is no gain in blaming others for their stalls. They realize they must invest in healing and continual learning. It is indeed a journey to arrive at the driver's seat.

2 CLAIM IT

"As I say yes to life, life says yes to me!"
—Louise Hay

You absolutely, unequivocally deserve to be happy and successful in your career. Lest you forget, I'm here to remind you. There's no need to remain miserable. Let me repeat that again. **There's no need to remain miserable in your career.** If you've been hanging out in misery for an extended period of time, now's the time to make changes. You deserve it. There are opportunities waiting for you. I give you permission to go after such opportunities.

TIP 1: GET YOUR MIND RIGHT

Create an affirmation to support the mindset shift needed here. If you have been telling yourself (by your actions) that you're undeserving of being happy in your career, you're going to have to spend a good amount of time undoing your handiwork. Affirmations repeated frequently send a message to our brains that we mean business. With time, you will realize that you will have a pep in your step when you think about your future.

Here are some valuable resources to support you as you build an arsenal of affirmations to rewire your brain.

—Louise Hay—*The Power Is Within You*
—Napoleon Hill—*Think and Grow Rich*
—Peter McWilliams—*You Can't Afford the Luxury of a Negative Thought*

TIP 2: CLAIM YOUR CAREER SUCCESS

Be the driver in your career. You deserve to be onboard with your career path/trajectory.

This tip is about the action required to claim your career success. You must begin to act in a manner that signifies you're in the driver's seat.

Some examples of this include diversifying your perspective to open yourself to the idea that you can take some action to restore your position to the driver's seat. I've encountered people who think there's absolutely nothing they can do to change their career situations and that is a falsehood. You might not be ready to make a bold change but certainly there's some change within your control. The key is doing the work to find those actions that will undoubtedly lead you to success.

I have a special message for mothers. This is because I was knocked for a loop when I had a child later in life. When I say loop, I mean by brain went amuck. I was stalled and actually didn't know my head from my tail, so to speak. It seemed like a good two years before I was able to resurface. I got lost, hanging out toward the bottom caring for my family and others to make sense of this transition. It was a heaping plate of feelings of insecurity and confusion.

Should you be in a similar space, I want you to still feel empowered to claim that you deserve a career too. You deserve to be in the driver's seat. Now I'm not saying that some of you aren't happy with the lot that you've been served. For me, I was ecstatic to be blessed with a beautiful daughter. However, I had this niggling feeling that my contributions were far from over and more widespread than parenting alone. Hence, I kept muddling my way through until I found something that held my interest and motivation to stay the course. I had to regain my confidence in myself and my abilities to succeed.

Find your one thing that will give you additional joy. Clarity came in the form of setting a solid example for my daughter and the younger generation. Every time I sit in the driver's seat, I think about the legacy I'm creating for my daughter. It isn't always easy because my work keeps me on the go. My little one is not always understanding of my hectic schedule, and there are many times when I'm feeling the mom guilt.

I do have to say I've been blessed along the way to meet strangers who give me free therapy just when I need it. There was the grandmother on the train who gave me an awesome pep talk. Then there was the mom who was a vendor at a tradeshow that I exhibited at. She gave me lots of stories of encouragement about her experiences and provided additional validation that I needed to continue the course. I share all that to say that you can start by claiming the driver's seat. You deserve it. People will show up to help you in your time of need.

Claim it and go forward and share your magic with the world.

TIP 3: DON'T BELIEVE THE VALUE HYPE

There is the movement around the word "value" that gets me a little ruffled in the career space. I've heard it a great many times. Don't show your face unless you have value to add. What's that now? Whether it's an interview, a performance review, or on social media, the core messaging is around challenging the offering that you bring to the table.

I'm here to tell you—stop listening to the hype around value. Especially if it's halting you from showing up and sharing yourself with the world. Many of us are hiding because we fear the judgment thrown upon us. We fear impostor syndrome. We fear people knowing that we aren't as brilliant as we project ourselves to be.

Can I give you a career tip? Don't let the word value hold you back. You have a right to show up and take your place in the driver's seat. Reframe your lens on the word value to think about how you package your valuable offerings.

TIP 4: MANAGE YOUR CAREER NARRATIVE

Manage your career narrative by leveraging the internet. I've forgotten where I learned this, but I was told to create a Google Alert on my name. This strategy allows me to be on top of any content that's posted online with my name attached. This includes content that others have posted about me.

One technique that I used to write my career narrative was tapping into publications that I admired to share my work. I've written for *Forbes*, *Glassdoor*, *Working Mother*, *Diversity Best Practices*, and more. You have an opportunity to submit your work for consideration. All they can say is no. You are resourceful enough to find the tools you need to succeed.

TIP 5: APPRECIATE YOUR DIVERSITY

Be ok with being a diverse human. We are all diverse individuals. Yet somehow we have been brainwashed into thinking we need to be more like others. I've been given so much advice on how to make myself palatable for others to easily digest. And I tried to fit in. Truly, I did. But guess what. I was unhappy.

The bottom line is that I have to be happy with me. And that means, I get to be in the driver's seat for my life. I get to embrace my diversity as a human. I have many skills that I bring to the table. And really I get to decide which ones I want to share with the world. I also get to decide what advice I want to take.

Build up trust in yourself so that you can make your own decisions.

TIP 6: DON'T GET DISTRACTED BY BLING

Don't let other people's career shine derail you. This means getting stalled by the appearance that others are winning, and you are not. This is about perspective. You can be motivated by other people's successes but what I don't want is for you to get stalled because someone else has won and you haven't won yet.

I like to tell my clients to pay attention to what others are doing. It's insight for your career journey. You can use the information to decide to incorporate a career opportunity into your plans. You can find a resource that you can tap into for learning. You can also find an opportunity for collaboration. Pay attention to roadmaps that are in your line of sight. The key is for you to home in on areas of interest and passion and move forward with what's best for your career.

TIP 7: PROTECT YOURSELF FROM NEGATIVITY

Attitude is everything, said the late motivational coach Keith Harrell. Check your attitude and your language. Are you using words that let you feel less than and keep you stalled in your career? Give yourself permission to have a good attitude about your career. I recommend a book called *Taming Your Gremlin* by Rick Carson. We all have gremlins that run amok in our minds telling us to continue playing small. We must ignore them and move on to creating our career legacy.

Speaking of playing small, limit your exposure to negative people. Negativity can be a deadweight. Know the saying, "Birds of a feather, flock together." Don't get drawn into negative drama. Be purposeful. Surround yourself with people who are excited in action and in walking in their purpose.

Suggested Actions

1. Write one affirmation message for claiming your position in the driver's seat.

2. Get your reading on.
   —*Attitude Is Everything* by Keith Harrell
   —*Taming Your Gremlin* by Rick Carson

3. Do an internet search on your name. Check for any negative commentary that might show up. Make a plan of how to address this (even if it means outsourcing it to an expert).

4. Set up a Google Alert for your name. Monitor alerts that come in.

5. Watch your social media intake and notice any feelings of disillusionment as you scroll.

6. Subscribe and listen to The Power of Owning Your Career Podcast. Visit https://www.simonemorrisenterprises.org/podcastbooks.

Action Plan

I plan to take the following actions to affirm my position in the driver's seat.

1.

2.

3.

I plan to leverage the following relationships to hold me accountable for the above actions.

I plan to accomplish these actions in this timeframe.

Notes

3 AUDIT

The auditing process is a self-reflective journey of what your experiences have been in your career to date. Home in on your emotional state as you reflect on your career.

- What's happening for you?
- What are you happy with?
- What are you not so happy with?
- Who are you happy with?
- Who are you not so happy with?

It's important that you give yourself the time to reflect on what's happening for you. Pay attention to what your days look like. Are there energy drains that are zapping your joy?

If so, what are those and what can you do to alleviate them?

Evaluate your findings, paying close attention to insights that bring about awareness.

TIP 8: GET HONEST WITH YOURSELF

Do an analysis of where you are in your career. This is worthwhile. I call it a brain dump of your career journey. See if you can spot any themes in your career chronicle.

To create effective change, you must document an honest depiction of where you are in our careers. Once you're able to see what's happening, you will then be able to zone in on the areas that require change.

Consider getting away to be alone with your thoughts. This doesn't have to be a financial burden. You certainly can grab a quiet room at the library and spend a day examining your insights. If need be, you can do several sessions. See if you can identify priorities as an outcome of this exercise.

Be sure to make this an ongoing step, as you will gain invaluable insights each time you undertake this process.

TIP 9: GET HEALED

Undoubtedly career wounds have happened to most of us. Stop blaming others for your career struggles. Take ownership of where you are in your career journey and make a plan to get where you want to go. This is an opportunity to invest in processing any wrongdoing that's weighing you down and keeping you stuck or stalled. To be successful and to move forward, I recommend leveraging a therapist to help you understand your journey and move past limiting beliefs that are holding you back.

Find a therapist who will provide objective listening in a nonjudgmental zone. Yes, there is sometimes negative stigma associated with mental health, but we can surely see the effects of proper treatment on thoughts and ideas that are hard to process.

I've taken advantage of employee assistance programs and therapists for my career success. Having a nonjudgmental person listen to your drama and provide insights on your journey is a game-changer.

Check out www.psychologytoday.com for recommendations of therapists. Of course, do your research. Get recommendations. Try a therapist. If it's not a fit, find another therapist you feel a good connection to. Don't be afraid to provide feedback on what's working and not working for you in a relationship with a therapist. Be your best advocate in this scenario.

TIP 10: UNDERSTAND THE LANDSCAPE

Read the writing on the wall. If your company doesn't see you as a high performer and you see yourself as one, then there's a disconnect. You are empowered to make the decision on how to move forward.

Either you **stay, investigate,** and build a **success squad;** or you **leave, find** and build **greener pastures.**

I once asked to look at my human
resources file (you are allowed to do that),
because I was convinced that there was some
dirt in it. There wasn't, but my mind was
telling me that there was something there
holding me back, and I truly needed to rule
that out of the equation.

It is key to pay attention to what's
happening. It's key to ask questions for
clarification. One question could be, "What's
the promotions process?" Other questions
might be, "What is holding me back from
securing a higher position in this company?
Will you provide mentoring and sponsorship
for me to become a stronger leader and get to
the next level within this organization?"

TIP 11: GET CLEAR ON THE UNWRITTEN RULES

I learned about unwritten rules during my
corporate days. You must pay attention to
what's not being said but is percolating in the
air when it comes to your career. Research the
unwritten rules for career success. Whatever
your career scenario, there are unwritten rules

for gaining career success. Start observing and asking questions to find out what those are.

TIP 12: STOP BEING COMPLACENT

That means if you're unhappy, do something about it. This ties back to the first goal I mentioned. Yes, other people can throw a monkey wrench into your career. The key is really what you do about it. Own your part of the equation and move forward. Get into an ownership mentality and start moving toward your dreams. Before you know it, you'll be there. "There" being where your dreams are fully realized.

Suggested Actions

1. Do some research on the unwritten rules in your career scenario. Document your findings and how you plan to use this new insight.
2. Do some reflection to home in on any writings on the wall you need to take action on.
3. Identify any career wounds that you have to heal from. How do you plan to address them? Whose help do you need to support your healing process?

Action Plan

I plan to take the following actions to affirm my position in the driver's seat.

1.

2.

3.

I plan to leverage the following relationships to hold me accountable for the above actions.

I plan to accomplish these actions in this timeframe.

Notes

4 PLAN IT

As someone with years of experience managing global projects, certified in project management, and teaching project management, I can tell you that planning is vital to your career success. If you don't spend the prerequisite time planning, then you will have to do a lot of course correcting or you run the chance of being unhappy with your current state. For the planning process, I recommend that you do the following.

- ➲ Create a yearly plan.
- ➲ Create a monthly plan in support of your yearly plan.
- ➲ Create a weekly plan in support of your monthly plan.

Learn how to create plans. It's not a bad idea to invest in a project management course as part of your development strategy. You can pick up the key concepts and then apply them to your career. What I want for you is to create plans to support your goals.

One tool you can use from the project management framework is a work breakdown structure (WBS). A WBS will help you come up with all the tasks required to complete your goal. Some things to think about in terms of your planning include timing and budget. Don't let that hold you back but factor that into your planning process. You can also check the Simone Morris Enterprises (SME) Academy for available training. I'll also refer you to my book, *Achievement Unlocked: Strategies to Set Goals and Manifest Them.* I cover action planning in the book.

TIP 13: SET GOALS FOR CAREER SUCCESS

Don't just wander idly. Set stretch goals for yourself. I run a workshop every year teaching practices for goal setting and action planning. I find it important to set goals and document them. They remind me of my journey. They remind me of my commitments. The results of my goals are concrete evidence of my career growth. In *The Power of Owning Your Career*, I talk about my passenger behavior of not being fully invested in the organization's goals and feeling like I constantly had to morph my authentic goals to a place that was palatable for the organization. After a while, I became disillusioned.

The morale of the story is to create and fight for your goals. If you don't agree, don't just go along with it. Talk it through until you find true alignment with your goals and the organization's goals that you feel passionate about. Even if that organization is your own business. This could also apply to other people who are calling the shots in your career (for example, spouse, family, or church).

TIP 14: CREATE A SOLID PLAN

Back in my corporate days, there was something called a professional growth plan. The concept was clever, and I went through the motions of completing the plan. Years later, I see what an immensely valuable tool it was in terms of career management. Today,

I'm intentional about carving out time to create an annual plan for my career.

Annually, I've offered my clients the opportunity to participate in a workshop called "My Life My Way." The workshop focuses on goal setting and action planning. It's always been well received.

As a reminder, your annual plan should include the following.

➲ Priority focus areas for your career (promotion, sponsorship, etc.).
➲ Strategic relationships that you want to build.
➲ A list of goals that you want to set for yourself.
➲ A monthly view of actions required to achieve goals outlined.

TIP 15: BREAK DOWN THAT PLAN

In *Achievement Unlocked: Strategies to Set Goals and Manifest Them*, I talk about how to go about creating plans to support the achievement of your goals. Here, I'm suggesting that you create multiple plans for success. Creating a further breakdown of your annual plan will make it more digestible and easier for you to act upon. Be sure to make updates along the way.

TIP 16: LEVERAGE TECHNOLOGY

Technology is ripe for the taking. Planning is a great area to leverage technology to own your career. Here are some online tools to consider.

- ➲ Asana—A way to manage and follow up on your goals.
- ➲ SmarterQueue—A way to manage your social media content without tying yourself to your computer to stay visible.
- ➲ LinkedIn—Leverage to showcase your thought leadership, build your strategic network, gain opportunities, and continue your professional development.

TIP 17: STOP DREAMING SMALL

It's so easy to dim our shine by playing smaller than our capabilities. We must give ourselves permission to start dreaming **big** dreams. It's scary. But as my favorite author, the late psychologist Susan Jeffers, says, we must remember that whatever happens, we can handle it. Big dreams give way to big growth. You owe it to yourself to dream about possibilities you want in your career.

One action I suggest doing is creating a list. Create two columns. One column will document what you have been talking about doing. You know the saying, "Talk is cheap." The second column will document what you've actually done. Use this as a guide to identify gaps and possibilities for what you plan to accomplish next in your career.

TIP 18: GAIN A COMPETITIVE ADVANTAGE

Keep your skills fresh. You cannot afford to avoid learning if you plan to remain competitive in your career. Make a professional development plan for yourself every year. Allow yourself time to think about how you plan to grow year after year. I have a template that you can leverage. Visit the Simone Morris Enterprises Store (www.simonemorrisenterprises.org/shop).

Invest your own money in your career growth. Whether that means a career coach, courses, conferences, etc. I say that because when you invest your own hard-earned dollars, you're truly invested in your career growth. If you're just depending on tuition reimbursement from your employer, then revisit that strategy. You deserve more and I'm here to help you get it.

Invest the time to learn. Learn daily. There are opportunities to learn everywhere.

Have a fluid professional development plan. This can help you grow in so many ways. You must track and consistently update where you think you need to focus on growing your development

TIP 19: BE A GOOD READER

My mom always says, "Nothing beats a good reader." Create a reading plan; make time to read to grow your skills. You will gain additional perspectives and ideas will percolate to allow you greater innovation.

Make time for reading. I know. It's tough. But you must. Find books that interest you and start a reading library. I've tried valiantly to listen to books on tape, but I fall short many times in that space. I love reading. Once I make the time for it, I find myself deeply engrossed in books.

Here are some career books that have been mentioned by guests on my podcast, The Power of Owning Your Career.

- *Radical Candor* by Kim Scott
- *Build your Dream Network* by Kelly Hoey
- *Brand You* by Hume Johnson
- *Reinventing You* by Dorie Clark
- *Real Talk* by Bridgett McGowen
- *Feel the Fear and Do It Anyway* by Susan Jeffers
- *Mindset: The New Psychology of Success* by Carol Dweck
- *Dare to Lead* by Brené Brown
- *The Universe Has Your Back* by Gabrielle Bernstein

- ➲ *Drop the Ball* by Tiffany Dufu
- ➲ *The Gutsy Girl Handbook* by Kate White
- ➲ *You're Not Lost* by Maxie McCoy
- ➲ *Personal History* by Katherine Graham

TIP 20: CREATE A REJECTION STRATEGY

Bolster your confidence by reframing the way you handle rejection. Here are some strategies to leverage when you have been rejected.

1. As life coach Iyanla Vanzant said, this too shall pass. Meaning the disappointment will dull with time. The sun does actually come out tomorrow. Cue smile!
2. After you finish thinking about how you're the cat's meow and your anger about said rejector not noticing your brilliance, tell yourself it's time to find the lesson for each rejection. Do a lessons-learned reflection and document what you'll do differently next go-round. It's entirely possible, you didn't put your best effort forward. Learn from that truth and move forward.

3. Not everyone is ready for your brilliance. Timing is key. Try again. Kudos to the those who say no thanks. Be sure to regroup and avoid giving up. When something is for you, it's for you. You just need to show up when the alignment is ready to happen.

4. Can't quote my Momma B enough, nothing beats a failure like a try. Remove the word failure and insert rejection. Repeat after me, nothing beats a rejection like another try!

5. This is a good time to read or start a success log that outlines all your successes. I do it on a yearly basis. Reminders about past wins automatically boost your self-confidence and provide evidence to stay the course.

6. There's more fish in the sea. Time to go fishing or learn, if you don't know how. Keep moving! Keep searching until you find your groove. Probably shouldn't say this, but I will anyway. Stella found hers, so why can't you? Comment if you need to know who Stella is!

7. Where can I find a mentor to help me with this? If this is something you truly

want, find someone who's done it
successfully and ask for his or her
guidance.

8. The mind is a terrible thing to waste.
   Educate yourself. Find out what
   education is available to bolster your
   capabilities. Perhaps a mastermind
   group will shine a light on
   opportunities to differentiate yourself.

9. As Viola Davis said in the movie *The
   Help*, "You is smart." Never forget that!
   You will find your tribe.

10. As spiritualist Don Miguel Ruiz said,
    don't take it personally. We all have a
    choice when we're shopping. We buy
    what meets our needs and works with
    our budget.

TIP 21: CREATE YOUR OWN OPPORTUNITIES

Stop waiting for folks to throw you a career
bone. Some folks are stingy with offering to
help you on your career journey. I'm going to
go out on a limb and say that many of us have
encountered someone who hasn't rolled out
the welcome mat to share their knowledge
with us.

The key is what do you do when you get a no or a roadblock? Sometimes you just have to roll up your sleeves and get creative in creating your own career opportunities. It might require free work but ensure that you're building your capabilities and content for your career narrative along the way. And before you know it, you'll have upped the ante, shifted perspective, and be sought after for your thought leadership. I've said it before and I'll say it again, don't rest on your laurels because opportunities aren't coming your way. Give yourself a kick in the pants (or skirt), you know what I mean, and start thinking about opportunities you can create on your own.

TIP 22: GET YOUR FINANCES IN ORDER

Some gaps that might exist include lack of emergency funds and long-term care planning. Hiring a financial planner is key to helping you navigate the process. I paid $3,000 to get my financial plan done. I was being cheap and held off for many years. That was the wrong decision. What a sense of relief I had when it was finally done. It finally validated that I had a good reserve and identified gaps that I needed to focus on.

This is a career tip that I stand by. Having a solid emergency fund gives you freedom when it comes to making decisions. It gives you freedom to dip in and take monies to further your educational interests. Perhaps tuition reimbursement isn't an offering. Perhaps you have to float money before it's reimbursed to you. Perhaps you have to pay yourself for a business that's not immediately yielding return. There are many reasons linked to career success that require you to invest in your financial future. Find someone you trust and get them on your success team.

Suggested Actions

1. Identify goals to accomplish in your career in the next three months, six months, and one year.
2. Complete an action plan for the goals identified above.
3. Select at least one technology that you plan to use to support your career success.
4. Pick three books that you plan to read/listen to in the coming months.
5. Create a professional development plan for the coming year.
6. Create a budget for career-related expenses.
7. Identify potential opportunities that you can go after.
8. Subscribe and listen to the Power of Owning Your Career Podcast. Visit https://www.simonemorrisenterprises.org/podcastbooks.

Action Plan

I plan to take the following actions to affirm my position in the driver's seat.

1.

2.

3.

I plan to leverage the following relationships to hold me accountable for the above actions.

I plan to accomplish these actions in this timeframe.

Notes

5 PERFORM

TIP 23: BUILD A LEARNING LAB

Consider building your own learning lab to innovate when it comes to your career. Use this space to try new things. Document lessons and continue to innovate. Experiment before you take your proverbial show on the road. It is, as the name suggests, a space to learn and grow with your career.

Get clear about what you need to learn, and use this space to pick up the new skills. Home in on your learning preferences. Then create a plan of action to surround yourself with what you need to continuously learn. I love the idea of carving out a space where you can carry out your learning. While you might have space to collect your books, you should consider broadening your perspective about what is welcomed in that space.

TIP 24: JUST DO IT

It's plain and simple. You have to take continuous action to get results. You cannot just sit on your laurels and expect success to happen in your career. You cannot just coast (stay complacent) and expect greatness.

I have discovered over the years that I must work for results. I must work on behalf of my dreams. I must work to create solid relationships (more on that later). I must work to find and create opportunities. At all times, I must be working toward my goal. Believe it or not, self-care is a part of that process. So, while working, don't burn yourself out. Recognize that you will need rest and rejuvenation to continue taking actions.

If you take no actions when it comes to your career, then your results will show just that. Take some action on your career daily. If you're unclear about your career goals, carve

out time to think through your career
requirements and then make some goals for
your career and create an action plan to
support the achievement of your goals.

Needless to say, I've got books to help you
on that. *Achievement Unlocked: Strategies to Set
Goals and Manifest Them* is all about goal setting
and action planning. It's a valuable resource to
support this process. If you want my handy
dandy autograph, you can purchase it on my
website. If you want it like yesterday, head to
Amazon and order your copy.

Please keep the Nike "Just Do It"
statement in the forefront of your mind. You
must take consistent action to get results.

Suggested Actions

1. What are the big ideas you have for your career?
2. What support do you need to keep going in your career?
3. Create a commitment letter that you can read when you stray from consistent actions that will help keep you in the driver's seat for your career.
4. Read *Achievement Unlocked: Strategies to Set Goals and Manifest Them.*

Action Plan

I plan to take the following actions to affirm my position in the driver's seat.

1.

2.

3.

I plan to leverage the following relationships to hold me accountable for the above actions.

I plan to accomplish these actions in this timeframe.

Notes

6 PARTNER

Collaborate with others for career success. Partnership is your key to success. Take career advice. Don't just sit on it. As the saying goes, do better when you know better.

TIP 25: TAP INTO MORE BRAINS

Join multiple mastermind groups to help you achieve your goals. Masterminds are a gold mine. The sooner you realize that, the better off you'll be. Masterminds help put you in good company to achieve your career results. They put you in a place where you can have access to the amount of accountability you need to be successful. A mastermind group is defined by Napoleon Hill as a meeting of the minds. It's an opportunity to get more people onboard to brainstorm your career challenges and it's a community to also leverage and celebrate your career success.

I'm currently in four mastermind groups. They are all with women business owners. I find the momentum and structure is a key career lever for me. I was always a great student. I consider myself to be a lifelong learner, so anything that contributes to learning for me is a positive investment of my time and energy.

TIP 26: EXPAND YOUR COMMUNITY

Join a networking group for results. At the recommendation of Kelly Hoey, I joined the Ellevate Network. I had been receiving invitations to join but was on the fence whether I wanted to make the financial investment. Kelly convinced me during our POOYC podcast interview. She outlined what a game-changing move it was for her career and I was sold. By the way, I don't think Kelly was selling but by the end of our conversation, I was sold. Visit my website https://www.simonemorrisenterprises.org/podcastbooks and check out Kelly's episode in season 1.

At the time of this writing, I've been in Ellevate for almost one year. The benefits thus far include the ability to showcase my leadership capabilities by leading an Ellevate Squad, increase the amount of networking I do regularly online and offline, meet new friends, and further hone my personal brand. Find a community that you believe in and get involved. Of course, do your research to make sure you find the community that you will soar in.

Join an online community. I give kudos to Kelly Hoey who told me about the Ellevate Network for women. It's an investment in my career growth. I've not just joined; I've made my presence known and I'm now branded as an Ellevate Expert. Ellevate offers women an online community that provides skill building and networking opportunities. I recommend you take advantage of this opportunity to get to build your network.

Do not just join and lurk. I see folks doing this on LinkedIn. They are afraid to show their brilliance. I'm going to remind you of the quote that I love from activist Marianne Williamson who is running for president of the United States in 2020. This quote is from her book, *A Course in Miracles.*

> *Your playing small does not serve the world. There's nothing enlightened about shrinking so that other people won't feel insecure around you. We are all meant to shine, as children do.*

Join a Facebook group. Contrary to popular belief, Facebook isn't just about being social. There are lots of opportunities to engage, meet new people, and land opportunities. I'm a part of several groups that are strictly about learning and growth opportunities. It does require you to be social. I say that because it's the obvious, but I know people on social media who detest being social and it shows in their engagement. They lurk and refrain from the true possibilities of engagement and collaboration.

TIP 27: FIND YOUR BFF

If you don't already have one, I want you to go out and find your career best friend or your business best friend. This is a supportive relationship to accompany you on your career journey. Over the years I've had a few career BFFs. For these relationships to work, you have to feel psychologically safe in the relationship to show up as your authentic self.

You will know how safe you feel when you consider the level of filtering you do in the relationship. If you have to filter your challenges and hardships, then keep searching for the right BFF relationship. You should be able to equally celebrate successes and challenges.

This is a valuable ally for the long haul. You should be able to speak with that person frequently so he or she can hold your hand for the journey.

TIP 28: MAKE TIME TO VOLUNTEER

Join an industry organization and volunteer for a leadership role. When I was first out of corporate, I was looking for a way to increase my experience in the human resources area. I will be forever grateful to the Southern Connecticut Chapter of the Society for

Human Resource Management for the opportunity to be its diversity director. It gave me hands-on experience in the area that I needed to build up. It was an opportunity for me to network, learn, and grow while demonstrating my leadership skills.

Your opportunity is waiting for you. You just have to identify it. Look around and find the organization that best aligns with your career goals. Find a leadership volunteer opportunity and raise your hand. Dive in and learn as much as you can. Do not assume the wallflower position.

Find the time to make this happen. This is key to build your driver-seat muscle.

TIP 29: LEARN TO SPEAK IN FRONT OF PEOPLE

It is critical that you develop public speaking skills, if you don't already have them. I was a member in Toastmasters for 10 years. It really was a game-changer for me because I was so afraid to get up in front of people and open my mouth. Today, I'm a professional speaker traveling the world and sharing my

message confidently on stages. Invest the
time.

Some organizations have their own
Toastmasters. If your organization doesn't
have one, it would be a good move to suggest
forming one. *Note: This is an opportunity to take
a leadership role and not expect someone else to do the
work. Don't shy away from making this happen.*

TIP 30: HIRE THE EXPERTS

Hire a career coach. Back when I was
floundering in my career, I thought that I
could just figure it out myself. I didn't. And
then I thought, I'd get help from the human
resource (HR)department. I did, but I didn't.
HR helped but not in the way that I needed.
You see, there was always a tie to the
organization and I never felt completely safe
in speaking my full truth. So, there were
variations of the truth.

I didn't know that I could hire a career
coach to partner with me for career success.
Sure, there's an investment of dollars but it's a
good investment in your career. If you're
struggling, there's help. LinkedIn provides an

opportunity for you to find professionals. It's called ProFinder. You can put a request out there with your needs and get some support. If I knew what I know today, I would have asked my organization to get me a career coach. I just didn't know. What's the harm in asking? The worst they could say is no.

Invest in a career coach. I'm not just saying this because I'm a career coach. Yes, I am that, but I actually believe in the power of coaching and how it can help you accelerate your career. I kick myself for not investing many moons ago in the corporate world. I was at a crossroad for such a long time. I didn't know that this was a key lever to be tapped for career success. I assure you that the right career coach can make a world of difference for your career.

TIP 31: UPGRADE YOUR RÉSUMÉ

Invest in your résumé. You need to sell yourself and a part of that package is the old-fashioned résumé. When I say old fashioned, I just mean the good old résumé. It works and some people live and die by the résumé.

For me, I see LinkedIn as the place that
everyone vets talent these days. However,
after they check you out on LinkedIn, they are
going to want to see that résumé, so go ahead
and get it done. This is another area of
investment for you. It is worth the money to
have someone present you in the manner
necessary to sell your capabilities before you
even show up for your opportunity
(interview).

TIP 32: UPLEVEL YOUR SKILLS

Whatever your profession, realize that you
must be updated about your industry. That
means investing resources (time, money, etc.)
into making this a reality. This might involve
going back to school for a degree program. It
could involve obtaining industry-specific
certifications that are designed to catapult
your career. Personally, I found the Project
Management Professional (PMP)®
Certification to be a game-changer in the
information technology world. Even today, it
is a credible certification.

If you're in business for yourself, take
advantage of certifications to move your

business forward. They provide educational opportunities, preplanned networking opportunities to build strategic relationships, access to funding, and more.

Some examples of this include the following.

- ➲ State level certifications (usually free of charge)
- ➲ Women's Business Enterprise National Council (WBENC) (cost involved)
- ➲ WEConnect International (cost involved)
- ➲ U.S. Department of Veterans Affairs (cost involved)
- ➲ National Minority Supplier Development Council (cost involved)
- ➲ Disability:IN (cost involved)

TIP 33: SAY YES

Say **yes** to career opportunities that scare the bejesus out of you. These opportunities are going to provide growth. Fight past the impostor syndrome and continue to take consistent action toward shining in this new area.

Start saying **yes** to building more relationships. That means more networking. You cannot afford to sit on your laurels and expect others to build strategic relationships for you. I learned the hard way about networking. I used to say no a lot, because I'm an introvert and networking can be exhausting for this former wallflower. Careful of that internal noise convincing you that networking is the big bad wolf.

TIP 34: FIND YOUR TRIBE

Find yourself some advocates, allies, and champions for your career. For many moons, I didn't know that I needed more people on my career team. Honestly, I thought I could do it alone. It took me a long time to learn that wasn't the best career strategy for growth.

Find your success tribe. You can start one by one. If you're on a project, start to network with the project leadership team. You will clearly know who's a fan of your work. When you spot those folks, you want to cultivate an authentic relationship with them. See if you can come up with five to ten people for your success tribe. Do not get tripped up by the numbers. I'm proud of you if you can come up with at least one person to add to your list. Don't beat yourself up. Be aware and make a plan to build out your success network if it's lacking.

TIP 35: DIVERSIFY YOUR NETWORK

Learn more about the complexity of the diversity definition. It's a lot more than what we typically consider (race, ethnicity, gender, sexual orientation, etc.). Know that there's an opportunity to find mentors, sponsors, and allies who are far more diverse than you imagined.

I want you to step out of your comfort zone and learn more about others and gain varied feedback that will undoubtedly be impactful to your career. Do your part on creating inclusive partnerships for career success. It doesn't have to be hard. Put yourself in an environment that is fertile and welcoming of inclusion.

TIP 36: LET YOUR VOICE BE HEARD

Share your story. Write an article. Publish a book. Create a podcast. Allow your voice to be heard by the masses. Of course, create goals and plans to make this a reality. I know you can do it. I did it.

Whenever you get an opportunity to create lasting change, to cause movement/impact for others, or to demonstrate your leadership skills, do not shy away from adding to the conversation. This is a game-changing opportunity for your career. Find a way to express yourself.

TIP 37: START DOING COFFEE CHATS

I first learned about coffee chats on Facebook. It was really great because it warmed me up to reframing how I viewed networking. Coffee chats are a great opportunity to further build your network. You schedule them for 20–30 minutes. They can be virtual and are about getting to know others without the pressure of asking for anything. Lean into building relationships over coffee/tea/hot beverage.

TIP 38: TRY OUT THAT GREEN THUMB

You must sow lots of seeds in your career to yield results. Being patient can be a challenge, but I have found that if I continue to nurture my seeds, they bloom in a way beyond my wildest expectations. Put your ideas out there and watch them bloom.

Suggested Actions

1. Find at least one mastermind group to participate in. Pay attention to how you are showing up and how you are being received in the mastermind group.
2. Find a confidante (BFF) who you can share career wins and challenges with.
3. Pick an organization that you want to volunteer for. Raise your hand for a leadership role.
4. Join Toastmasters to build confidence and public speaking skills.
5. Hire a career coach to partner with you on your career success.
6. Identify potential sponsors/advocates who can and are willing to support your career growth.
7. Become a mentor
8. Say yes to at least one ask that scares you.
9. Build your inclusion muscles by putting yourself in scenarios that increase your cultural competency.
10. Update your résumé.
11. Subscribe and listen to The Power of Owning Your Career Podcast. Visit https://www.simonemorrisenterprises.org/podcastbooks.

Action Plan

I plan to take the following actions to affirm my position in the driver's seat.

1.

2.

3.

I plan to leverage the following relationships to hold me accountable for the above actions.

I plan to accomplish these actions in this timeframe.

Notes

7 PROMOTE

TIP 39: CREATE A PERSONAL BRAND

Do not just hang your hat on the company brand. Your identity can get lost in your company brand. If that's you, then that's ok. Just know, now is the time to make a change to create your own personal brand. My identity was lost in a corporate brand for a long time. I lived and breathed the organization. I didn't realize it until I left the organization. When people saw me, they saw the organization. Kudos to the organization for solid employer branding. However, it proved to be a detriment for me.

I began dissociating myself from the corporate brand so that I could start from scratch and build my personal brand. I had to take some time to discover what that personal brand was. I had to trust my instinct and allow myself the time to allow my brand to surface. It's been a journey that has been tweaked and will probably continue to be tweaked.

Big brands do it too. Look at the Coca-Cola brand and how it's morphed over time. Companies morph. Why shouldn't your brand morph? These days my brand is about putting women in the driver's seat for their careers in addition to teaching organizations that inclusion matters and that they can do more to create inclusive humans. A tall order indeed.

Dr. Hume Johnson wrote the book *Brand You*. That's a resource you can tap into. Invest dollars into creating your personal brand. Once you have the brand figured out, weave it into your career narrative. Validate that others see your brand. Show up and consistently wear your brand. Hire a brand strategist if you need to. Know that your brand will morph. I hired a graphic designer on Upwork.com to work with me on creating my brand identity.

She's solid. I think you'll agree if you take a look at my website and marketing collateral. My next step will be to order a nametag with my branding identity.

TIP 40: LEVERAGE A NETWORKING BRIEF

Give the person you're networking with an opportunity to get to know you and outline your asks. Oftentimes, people are willing to help us, but they don't know what we want. Equally, they can be scared off if we're gung-ho with what we want and it's a me, me, me conversation. Strive to make it a win-win relationship. I know it can be hard. If you mess up, forgive yourself, and course correct for success.

TIP 41: TOOT! TOOT!

My Aunt Louise sends cards to celebrate each occasion. What I love about her cards is not only the beautiful stickers she adds to brighten our days. She also sends copies of her accomplishments. How fabulous is that! It's really terrific because she's 75. You're never too old to toot your own horn.

Here are some ideas of how you can begin to toot your own horn. Remember you are your best advocate.

⮑ Start showing up on LinkedIn, despite those advising you to only share valuable content. Do not just show up as a lurker. Join the conversation and share your perspective. Lose the filtering. Be brave.

⮑ Join Toastmasters if you need to learn how to use your voice. Gain confidence and then revisit the task of tooting your own horn.

⮑ Start telling people what you're doing. If you're working for someone else, do this internally and externally.

⮑ Write an article for an industry publication.

⮑ Volunteer to speak in a highly visible area.

⮑ Write a press release highlighting an accomplishment and share it with local media.

TIP 42: OVERHAUL YOUR SOCIAL PROFILE

Invest in your LinkedIn profile. I know. More money. I'm telling you though, this investment is going to pay off. You want to show up on LinkedIn in the right way. If you're a talented copywriter, editor, etc., then by all means go forward and write your winning copy. If it's taking you forever and a day to complete your profile, go ahead and outsource the job. Leverage Fiverr.com or Upwork.com to hire someone to do your profile for you. You can also leverage a résumé writer from your networks that you trust. What I care about is that you're buttoned up on this front.

Embrace LinkedIn as a tool for career success. This underutilized tool is a goldmine for career success. You cannot afford to not attend the LinkedIn party. I'm saying party and it's not really a party, so to speak, but my point is you need to show up in the space. Not only do you need to show up, you need to make your presence known. That means a professional profile photo, sharing of content, building of your connections, and sharing of your expertise.

Invest in your LinkedIn presence. Pay for the professional photo. Pay for the profile rewrite, if your profile isn't getting results. The key here is to ensure that your brand is high quality and that you mean business when it comes to your career.

TIP 43: BUILD YOUR ASK MUSCLES

Build your ask muscles. Do you know how to ask in your career? You must learn how to ask for what you want. This can be a difficult one, but the Bible says, "Ask, and you will receive" (Luke 11:9, Good News Translation).

Perhaps you've been networking and hoping that all the value you're providing will just magically yield results. Or, perhaps you're one of the lucky ones who doesn't have to worry about this issue.

TIP 44: SPEAK OUTSIDE YOUR ORGANIZATION

Volunteer to speak at a conference, meeting, or event. If you don't want to be the main speaker, volunteer to be a panelist. How about being a guest on a podcast? This is a way for you to build and demonstrate your expertise (that is, thought leadership). Go for it. Someone is waiting to say yes.

TIP 45: STAY VISIBLE

Consider the following. Does your favorite brand hide from you? If you're a Starbucks fan, can you find it? Are the stores visible to you? What about McDonalds? What about Apple? What about Verizon? Old Navy? Marshalls? Michaels? I think you get the gist. These brands don't hide because if they do, they will lose their clients and no longer be in business.

Do not hide at your desk. Do not shy away from opportunities. You must be visible so that people are aware of your brand and what it represents.

Suggested Actions

1. Invest in revamping your LinkedIn profile. Show up in a way that supports the way you want your brand to be received.
2. Identify a list of three game-changing things you need to ask for in your career.
3. Reach out to organizations to volunteer. Ask to be a speaker, panelist, or moderator.
4. Complete a networking brief outlining the asks you have for the people you plan to network with.
5. Identify ways you plan to share your career successes. Toot! Toot!
6. Subscribe and listen to The Power of Owning Your Career Podcast. Visit https://www.simonemorrisenterprises.org/podcastbooks.

Action Plan

I plan to take the following actions to affirm my position in the driver's seat.

1.

2.

3.

I plan to leverage the following relationships to hold me accountable for the above actions.

I plan to accomplish these actions in this timeframe.

Notes

8 SELF-CARE

TIP 46: TAKE CARE OF YOURSELF

Treat yourself well. This journey requires stamina. Be kind to yourself. There are disappointments, rejections, etc. Find the outlet that helps you to bounce back when you get the no answers. Suspend your judgment of yourself.

Fuel up. You will need it. Take advantage of opportunities to sleep. If you're not getting your seven hours, invest in finding out what's your sleep block. Do not ignore this problem. It might take some time but fix whatever's bothering you so you can get back to your sleep.

This seems like a no-brainer, but I can tell you, it's one often forgotten. Where are you on your list? Are you at the top or are you at the bottom because of the plethora of responsibilities under your remit? You must fill your tank so that you can drive the distance. While you're at it, fill it with premium octane so you can move the distance.

I've operated on empty many times, so I know it's not a great feeling. You will notice if you're constantly drained because your attitude will be affected. You will be short-tempered and easily irritated. You will have difficulties concentrating. You will feel tired or the opposite—wired and perhaps experiencing insomnia.

My good friend Ingrid, who's a nutritionist schooled me about the term adrenal fatigue. You might have that. Check out the book *Adrenal Fatigue* by James L. Wilson as a resource. Heck, you might even want to call Ingrid for a free consultation (www.fulllifenutrition.com).

TIP 47: FIND YOUR PEACE

Is it meditation? Is it yoga? What gives you great joy? Find it and keep doing it. Let it be your go-to when you're feeling depleted. I know this is a no-brainer but oftentimes we forget about what really gives us joy. I'm giving you permission to go back to those places to ensure your happy tank is filled up.

One strategy that I use for finding my peace is listening to my gut feelings. They are a beacon to highlight whether your life is off-kilter. Grant yourself permission to do what gives you peace continually.

TIP 48: GIVE YOURSELF PLAYTIME

Don't lose sight that you're entitled to have fun in your career and life. Truly, you can be so focused on your goals, that you're missing out on fun. Find a way to incorporate fun into your career goals.

My four-year-old daughter is teaching me how to play again. Honestly, I forgot how to play. She has me doing puzzles, expanding my imagination, answering questions, watching her and her friends frolic during playdates, exploring new places, and more. How wonderful to revisit the childlike mindset where you staved off worrying about your career and life. Try it. I know television producer and writer Shonda Rimes mentioned doing just that in her journey.

TIP 49: CHECK THE TIRE

Check your life, for that matter. I remember the word well-rounded. We want a well-rounded student. A well-rounded employee. The meaning behind this was that they wanted somebody who had varied experiences. So, I want you to have varied experiences and not have your wheel be lopsided.

In the coaching world, the wheel of life is a tool that's used to look at your life and ensure that you're not limping along. The analogy is to a tire, where your tire won't run smoothly if there's an area lacking attention. As women, it can be tough to find balance as motherhood enters the equation.

TIP 50: KEEP IT REAL

How many of us have been taught to stifle our emotions in the workplace? Never let them see you cry? I know I received that message loud and clear. I boasted proudly that there was only one moment in my career that almost brought me to tears in public. I suffocated those emotions by excusing myself to regain my composure.

Looking back, I can see that wasn't the healthiest approach. Emotions in a work setting seem to be such a taboo. I think there are also cultural differences at play. It is ok to let your humanity shine through. Hopefully there's a compassionate person on the other side. If there isn't, don't torture yourself. Chalk it up to—you guessed it—being human.

Suggested Actions

1. Identify your fun factor. What are three fun things you can incorporate in your life?
2. Get specific by identifying your top three priority focus areas.
3. Invest in an activity that brings you peace (yoga, exercise, meditation, sleep, etc.).
4. Subscribe and listen to The Power of Owning Your Career Podcast. Visit https://www.simonemorrisenterprises.org/podcastbooks.

Action Plan

I plan to take the following actions to affirm my position in the driver's seat.

1.

2.

3.

I plan to leverage the following relationships to hold me accountable for the above actions.

I plan to accomplish these actions in this timeframe.

Notes

9 CELEBRATE

TIP 51: CELEBRATE YOUR CAREER JOURNEY

This is vital for your career success. Don't belittle your accomplishments or, worse, keep them the best secret in town. Stand on the rooftops and shout your success. Ok, well, maybe that's a big stretch. However, I do believe in the value of tooting your own horn.

This is a form of celebration. When I completed my first book, my sister Michelle asked me about a book-signing party to celebrate my success. It sounded like a great idea but frankly I was too tired and went on to the next goal.

The second time I released a book, she said, "You have to have a book signing. I will help you. All you have to do is pick a date." And off we went. I have to tell you that it was one of the most memorable highlights of my career to date. I call that the power of accountability. She held the vision, shared it with me, I bought into it, and she held me accountable. I'll be forever grateful to her for this gift.

I'd like to offer a challenge to move past your comfort zone and try on celebrations. I know. I know. Maybe you're not the celebratory type. If that sounds like you, consider a form of celebration that would feel right to you. Perhaps it's just giving yourself a pat on the back and heading out to dinner with someone special. You deserve it for all the time, effort, and work you've put into your career journey. Go ahead. Pause now and repeat this affirmation after me.

"Congratulations, _____ (insert your name here)! You're amazing. You did a great job and I'm proud of you."

How did that feel?

TIP 52: HOLD AN ACCOUNTABILITY PARTY

Don't wait for the completion of your career to celebrate your success. You are empowered to have your celebration upfront, during, and after reaching your goals.

Presumably you've found some partners along the way to support your career goals. Now is the time to recognize your accountability team for ensuring you were successful in your career. Plan some time to get together with your accountability buddies to celebrate one another's successes.

I've done a celebratory lunch with my accountability buddies Joy and Lesslie. They took the journey with me to reach a career goal, and we acknowledged and celebrated that journey. Another example was a simple exchange of text messages and phone calls with my BFF and accountability buddy Bridgett.

Each win was shared and although we didn't go out to a meal for every celebratory moment, we stopped to acknowledge key success moments in our careers. I also share with my loved ones.

Don't dim your brilliance. Bask in the glow of accomplishing the wins in your career.

Suggested Actions

1. Invite your accountability partner to coffee to celebrate a recent success.
2. Share a recent success via social media.
3. Share your career success with an online community that you're part of.
4. Pat yourself on the back for a job well done.
5. Indulge in your favorite dessert as a reward for your career success. Responsibly, of course.
6. Create a list of rewards that you want to give yourself when you achieve your career goals.

Action Plan

I plan to take the following actions to affirm my position in the driver's seat.

1.

2.

3.

I plan to leverage the following relationships to hold me accountable for the above actions.

I plan to accomplish these actions in this timeframe.

Notes

10 CONCLUSION

True career success can be gained by designing your own custom formula for owning your career. There will be many who demonstrate what's possible for your career. The key is to embrace your role in the process.

This book has provided 52 practical tips, bonus advice, and additional resources to help you succeed in taking ownership of your career. It is my hope that these tips will help you to create much needed shifts in your career. Shifts that move you from the passenger to the driver's seat in your career.

After all, you only have one life and it is indeed yours to live, so seize your career wheel and make it a worthwhile one.

11 BONUS ADVICE

I've had some stellar guests on The Power of Owning Your Career Podcast. Below are ten pieces of career advice on what it takes to own your career.

1. Own who you are, what you do, and how you make magic show up in everything you do.
   —Bridgett McGowen, CEO, BMcTALKS

2. Listen to your inner self to identify where your passion and empathy lie. That's the cause you should pursue.
   —Hetal Parikh, president and cofounder, Rangam Consultants Inc.

3. Get clear about who you are and what value you bring to the table.
   —Dr. Hume Johnson, branding and communications consultant, professor of communications, Roger Williams University, Rhode Island

4. You don't owe anyone anything. Step into this mindset. Know who you are and take pride in that, mistakes and all. Live your life full-out.
   —Rukmini Reddy, VP of engineering, Abstract

5. Let go of the employee mindset. You are brand! Don't discredit the small things you do every day and embrace your passions and purpose and apply it to you career goals.
   —Kanika Tolver, CEO and founder, Career Rehab, LLC

6. Set up a steering committee of trusted advisors.
   —Ingrid Arredondo, nutritional therapist, CEO, Full Life Nutrition LLC

7. Be patient. Know yourself and what fulfills you. Keep moving forward. Narrow your focus.
   —Julie Ann Sullivan, *The Queen of Culture*, best-selling author, podcast host

8. Take 10 minutes a day to really think about what it is that you want to do, how you are going to get there, and who and what resources you will use to develop your skills.
   —Shirell Gross, founder and president, Measure of Ambition LLC

9. Learning to be comfortable with what might feel uncomfortable is how we grow. "Go out on a limb; that is where you find the fruit."
   —Marie Mann-Oliveras, human resources executive

10. Don't be afraid of failure—it's an amazing learning opportunity.
    —Shannon Malkin Daniels, CEO and Founder, encaptiv

12 GET YOUR CAREER BREAKTHROUGH

If you are ready to get in the driver's seat, I'm ready to work with you now.

My Career Breakthrough Program is designed to give you time to focus on creating a career that is designed on your terms. In this program, you soak up inspiration and confidence to soar in your career. Learn strategies to build/improve your personal brand.

You gain access to inspirational leaders who share actionable career advice. You walk away with a professional headshot to use to uplevel your brand. Best of all, you start to plan for that career you've been dreaming of.

The program includes these benefits.

➲ Half-day career strategy intensive session
➲ Career education sessions
➲ One-on-one career coaching
➲ Accountability support
➲ And more . . .

To learn more, schedule your career breakthrough call today at www.careerbreakthroughcall.com.

ABOUT THE AUTHOR

Simone Morris is CEO of Simone Morris Enterprises LLC, a certified minority and women-owned business enterprise. She is an award-winning diversity and inclusion leader and a consultant and speaker committed to diversifying the workplace, and training women and emerging leaders to take true leadership positions in all aspects of their lives.

She has a background that includes over two decades in corporate America, spanning information technology, commercial strategy, and human resources. She holds an MBA from the University of Connecticut. Her technology background has served her well, embedding strong project management acumen that allows her to educate and create transformational results for her clients.

She shares her message across various platforms (for example, *Forbes, Medium, Thrive Global, Glassdoor, Leadercast, SmartRecruiters, Social Hire, Diversity Best Practices, Profiles in Diversity Journal,* and *BambooHR*). She is also the author of *The Power of Owning Your Career: Winning Strategies, Tools and Tips for Creating Your Desired Career,* and *Achievement Unlocked: Strategies to Set Goals and Manifest Them.*

She resides in Connecticut with her family.

To gain additional career tips, subscribe to Simone's Monthly Newsletter by visiting www.simonemorrisenterprises.org

LEARN HOW TO WORK WITH SIMONE

There are ample opportunities to work with Simone Morris, including the following.

- ➲ Hire Simone as a career coach.
- ➲ Book Simone as a keynote speaker for your conference, meeting, or event.
- ➲ Book Simone to support professional development initiatives for your employee (or business) resource group.
- ➲ Hire Simone to conduct learning webinars.
- ➲ Hire Simone to moderate your panels.
- ➲ Hire Simone to be a career expert panelist.
- ➲ Purchase online learning via the Simone Morris Enterprises Academy.

Contact Information
smorris@simonemorris.com
929-399-6241
www.simonemorris.com
www.simonemorrisenterprises.org

BUY MORE BOOKS BY SIMONE E. MORRIS

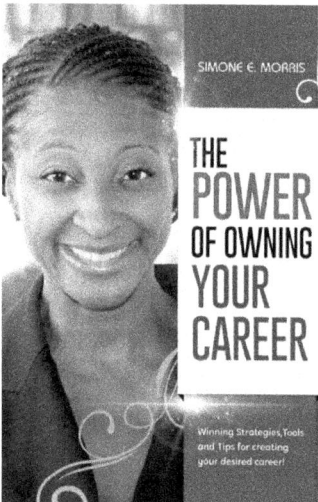

The Power of Owning Your Career book is a guidebook for career success. It's a chronicle of leaders and their journeys to the driver's seat.

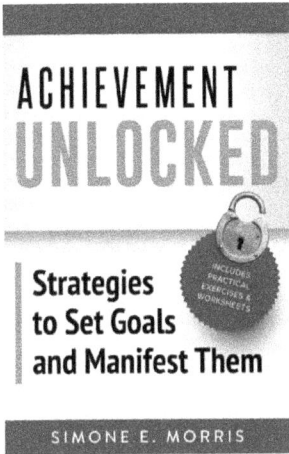

Achievement Unlocked: Strategies to Set Goals and Manifest Them is a book about the goal setting and action planning process. Get practical exercises and worksheets to support your growth.

www.ingramcontent.com/pod-product-compliance
Lightning Source LLC
Chambersburg PA
CBHW071707210326
41597CB00017B/2373

9 780999 438459